LEARNING SOCIAL FACTOR HOW CHANGES

ORGANIZATIONAL BEHAVIOR

JOHN LOK

Contents

Preface

Introduction

How social change influences human behavioral change ? Why human behavior may be influenced by social change? Our individual behavior whether can be influenced to bring negative or positive attitude by social change? I shall attempt to indicate cases to explain whether our individual behavior can be influenced to changed by social environment change. Readers can have more understand how and why social change may influence our behavior in possible as well as social changing behavior may influence organizational employment behavioral change. Behavioral economy is one useful and fun social subject. Behavioral economists ususally research how and why human behaviors may influence economy growth or recession, or how and why economy environment changing factor may influence human behavior changes.

In my this book, I shall attempt to explain how and why ecommerce may be one kind network human job. Also, I shall indicate reasons to explain why human network behavior may bring direct or indirect influences to economy growth or recession in our global societies in macro and micro economy view. Why leisure changing environment may influence human behavior , even economic environment changes. I shall indicate cases to explain any possible human social activities may bring direct or indirect influences to cause our social economic growth or recession in consequency in possible. How social changing behavior influences organizational employment behavior changes. I hope that my readers can feel more understanding whether what real meaning of behavioral economy is the relationship between our behaviors and our economy as well as how social changing may influence organizational employment behavioral change.

Prologue

Contents

CHAPTER I

How social change influences organizational recruitment behavior

Recruitment and selection – The most important HR function

Recruitment and selection process is one of the most important HR function which makes a great impact on the revenue growth and the profit margins of a company as compared to other tasks such as retention, on-boarding, leadership development and managing talent. In addition, recruitment and selection process is also more important than restructuring the organization, work/ life balance and strategic HR.

Why a proper recruitment and selection process important?

Most HR departments use the major portion of their effort and money to manage employees, and as a result, they are usually unable to adequately fulfill the organization's hiring needs. Inevitably, organizations end up hiring too many or too little employees to fill vacancies.

If the number of employees in a department exceeds the need, then the organization will suffer a loss as the cost of maintaining that department increases in comparison to its earnings. On the other hand, if a key position is left vacant then that causes losses too as it directly results in reduced corporate revenue. Today, we need a shift from the traditional concept of hiring that treats all job vacancies equally to one that prioritizes each vacancy depending on criticality. A perfect balance of employees and work needs to be maintained in a company. In addition, a job recruiter needs to ensure that only the most skillful and competent people should be selected for the jobs. The costs of hiring an inappropriate candidate can be enormous for an organization.

Implications of week hiring

Hiring can be considered weak when the new hire failure rate is high. If the new hires are terminated or voluntarily quit within first few months, regardless of their performance, then the new hiring can hardly be called a success. Unsuccessful hiring not only forces you to rehire for the same position but also adds to the cost of damage sustained by the bad hire.

The number of days lost in key projects and the cost of delays can be the direct results of weak hiring and low-quality recruitment process. Weak hiring not only causes losses in terms of project delays but can also help miss strategic opportunities. There is no guarantee that candidates who performed well in the recruitment exercise will do well in performing organizational functions. Therefore, it is important that new employees are given orientation into a company's functions before they are given important tasks.

Recruitment is, therefore, one of the most important of HR functions, which requires careful planning from start to finish. Also, a job recruiter needs to have business acumen, far-sightedness to judge organizations growth requirements and astute judgement. Most organizations, for smooth functioning of their HR functions, are now days purchasing recruitment and talent management software to manage their recruitment and selection process more efficiently.

Social change influences organizational HR strategic plan changes

Management is defined as a set ofilizing of process on human and non-human resources to efficient and effectively achieves the organizational goals (Davidson, Simon, Woods & Griffin. W. 2009, p.5). These processes are planning, organizing, leading and controlling. According to Robbins. P., Bergman and Stagg (1997, p.8) & Bateman. S. and Sneel. A. (2009, pp. 19 & 20), planning is about analyzing current circumstances, forecasting future, defining goals, establishing strategy and determining the resources needed; organizing is coordinating the resources by knowing what task need to be done, distribute jobs to group of people and allocating the resources; leading is to enhance the performance of people by directing, communicating and motivating all the parties involved;

controlling is monitoring activities as what has planned and made and necessary modification. However, these are not the only responsibilities of managers, as they have to perform managerial roles, apply management perspectives and deal with management challenges.

Firstly, managerial roles need to be played by managers when they are performing their jobs. Three of the managerial roles are interpersonal roles, information roles and decision roles. Interpersonal roles are about the communication, interaction and relation with people. It is divided into figurehead, leader and liaison. Mullins. J. (2007, pp.424) states that figurehead role is regard to manager formally denotes as symbol and representative of company in giving speech for companyâ€™s activities, etc. Moreover, leader role is the responsibility of managers to lead and motivate their underlings such as giving incentive to the workers if the organization reaches their goal. The relationship of managers with people out from their organization, such as personally promote their product to the public, is known as liaison role.

In addition managerial roles, information roles is about gathering of information and providing them to the people. It is classified into monitor, disseminator and spokesperson. Monitor role consists of the action of managers to achieve information from newspaper or environmental events to keep an eye on customers and competitors; disseminator role is that managers have to be able to share the information which have been collected with people in the organization, for instance, through e-mail; spokesperson role is the sharing of information with people outside their organization through the annual meeting or press conference (Williams. R. 2009, p. 20). Decisional roles involve managers making of decisions and establishing of strategies while obtaining and sharing of people. It is divided into entrepreneur, disturbance handler, resource allocator and negotiator. In Mullins. J. (2007, pp.425), entrepreneurial role is managersâ€™ function to introduce new ideas and plans to improve their current circumstances, for example, while financial crisis; disturbance handler role is responsibility of managers to react to unpredictable or unfavorable events; resource allocator role is managers decide on how the resources available can be efficiently allocated to parties involved in a program; negotiator role is participation of managers in negotiate with customers or suppliers in trade. Hence, these managerial roles are things that managers need to be provided with.

Other than that, managers also have jobs to apply some essential management perspectives, classical management perspective and quantitative management perspective, to the organization. Classical management consists of scientific management and administrative management. Scientific management involves using of scientific method to improve the productivity of each labour, such as implement a more efficient way for each part of the production process and give better payment to those who have produce higher output (Davidson et al. 2009, p.41). Whereas, administrative management is more emphasize on managing the whole organization (Davidson et al. 2009, p.41). Some of the principles advocate by Henri Fayol was division of labour, discipline, remuneration, stability, etc. For example, division of labour is to divide tasks to specific worker to make the process more effective.

Furthermore, there are 2 components, management science and operations management in quantitative management perspective. Management science is about ââ‚¬Å“uses mathematical modeling to simplify the representation of systems processes and relationships, often to predict human resource needs or product designââ‚¬? (Davidson et al. 2009, p.51). It is basically means that everything can be represented in mathematical form so that it is easier for people to analyze. After that, operational management is to apply management science by going through a transformation process of converting inputs into final goods and services (Davidson et al. 2009, p.41) & (Robbins., P., Bergman & Stagg 1997, p.713). For instance, good operational management may help the company to produce and deliver goods to their customers in an efficient and saving cost way. Thus, these are some theory that managers to do in the production process.

Besides that, managers will also have to deal with some challenges such as technology transformation and globalization of business. These challenges may be a threat for the organization, but it also could be an opportunity for them. In technology transformation, it is important for managers to pay attention to it as technology can help improve quality of products, enhance productivity and enable easier achievable of information. For example, a car manufacture company can use the most advance technology to provide their customers with better facilities so that they can satisfy their customers and have a stronger predominance in the market than their competitors.

Other than that, globalization of business is also one of the challenges as political and economical changes in other countries may affect every business around the world. At the same time, organization may seize the opportunities to extend globally. For example, in 1970s and 1980s, Japan began to export and manufacture and distribute their product in markets within Europe and United State. They begin to improve the quality of their product and soon their product became the world- class quality standard in the market (Cook. W. & Hunsaker. L. 2001, p.26). Hence, how the managers deal with these challenges is very important for the organization.

In conclusion, we can see that managerial roles, management perspective and management challenges are some of the tasks that managers need to do other than planning, organizing, leading and controlling. To be good managers, these are things that they are essential to know and they should be able to master them. With these skills, they could help the organization get rid of rumors; bring appreciable benefit to the organization in long run.

CHAPTER II

How social changing factor influences organizational HR development plan changes

Social change influences organizations feel internal staff transfer or promotion plan changes

Human resource development is defined by Heathfield (2010) "as the framework for helping employees develops their personal and organizational skills, knowledge and abilities". Human resource development involves using a range of learning and training techniques and strategies to change the work related behavior and attitudes of an employee (Megginson et al 1999) and it also engages in performance management in other to ensure that people can do things well or do new and better things (Gibbs 2008).

This study is aimed to analyze the purpose of Human resource development and also using this aims to analyze how it helps organizations achieve sustained competitive advantage by using organization example.

AIM OF HUMAN RESOURCE DEVELOPMENT

Human resource development according to Philbeam and Corbridge (2002:285) "is concerned with enhancing organizational performance through effective development and deployment of organizational members". To enhance performance, a human resource developer has to ensure that the individuals in the organization has the knowledge, expertise and the right attitudes to execute their work (Swanson and Arnold 1996), also, human resource development aims at ensuring that the organization has the skilled, committed and well-motivated employee it needs to sustain competitive advantage by focusing on processes that develop skills, knowledge and the attitude of the employee (Swanson Arnold 1996), such as training, developing, learning, educating and mentoring the employee (Stewart and McGoldrick 1996), and also by “identifying and improving the skills and motivation of employees” (Philbeam and Corbridge 2002:284).

In other to ensure that the organization as the right people to sustain competitive advantage, Human resource development engage in the following training, learning, development of the individual and mentoring but before the Human resource developer makes a decision on how to train, develop, teach or mentor the employee they need to have a concept on performance management in other to see how training and development will improve the effectiveness of the employee and to know what aspect in the performance of the employee needs to be trained in other to meet the goals and values of the organization (Megginson et al 1999).

Performance management

Performance involves what an employee does in carrying out their duty (Mathis and Jackson 2003). Before performance is managed the performance needed by the organization should be identified in other to achieve their goals which in most organization is linked to the mission statement of the organization so that the performance can be managed in line with the organizational values and some organization will manage the performance in line with the business strategy of the organization that are required in the business context to be competitive (Torrington et al 2005). Performance management is defined by Armstrong (2009:618) as “a systematic process for improving organization by developing the performance of individuals and teams”. Torrington et al (2005) cited Mabey and Salaman (1995) who defined performance management as “establishing a frame work in which the performance by individual can be directed, monitored, motivated and rewarded and whereby the links in the cycle can be audited”. “Human resource development is a means to an end. That end is usually acknowledged to be getting better results from the organization, teams and individuals by understanding and managing performance within an agreed framework of planned goals, objectives and standards"(Gibb 2008).

Every organization wants an employee that performs well in their duty it is believed that an effective performance management scheme can make the likely of good performance to occur (Mathis and Jackson 2003). Performance management goes beyond the ability and motivation of the individual it involves how goals are clearly identified in enabling the employee to understand what is expected of them in the area of their job and to set their priorities (Torrington et al 2005). Performance management scheme involves processes that can be used to encourage, motivate, evaluate, reward and identify the performance of the employee (Mathis and Jackson 2003). Performance management develops the capacity of the employee to meet, exceed and to achieve their full potential for the benefit of the organization as well as themselves, it can also serve as the basis for self development and ensure that the support and the guidance need by the employee to develop and improve is available (Armstrong 2009).

Megginson et al (1999) discuss the work of Ulrich (1998) who was of the view that performance management is what employees and managers do at work, that the way they act and interact is crucial to the success of the organization and in doing this it will raise the profile and value of training as a strategy for achieving competitive advantage.

Training

Staffs are important resources to an organization in other to achieve economic and effective performance, in other to ensure that an organization has staffs that are capable of career advancement into the role of a specialist or a manager an organization needs to engage in adequate training (Mullins 2002). Training is defined as "learning and development undertaken for the purpose of supporting development and maintenance of operational capability in employment: skills for work and in work, on-job or off-job, to enable effective performance in a job or role" (Gibb 2008:5).

Training involves modifying skills, knowledge and abilities through learning to achieve effective performance (Wilson 2005). It is believed that training makes an individual become effective managers as a result of their techniques having impact on inherent abilities, competence and skills (Hunt and Baruch 2003). Training makes the employees believe that the organization is committed to them and in securing their future in the organization which motivates the employees to Work harder and better (CIPD 2008), and it also develops the expertise of the individual in other to increase their performance in the organization (Swanson). Training and development is "equipping the employee with the right skills, knowledge and competence to maximize performance" (Philbeam and Corbridge 2002).Also, training improves the level of the organization as well as the individual competence and it's also a key element in improving organizational performance (Mullins 2002). Competence is defined by Stensgaard (2004) "as the combination of awareness, skills, knowledge and abilities that enables an individual to perform a job to the standards required for successful job performance". Competence is more than learned knowledge, skills and abilities but involves motives, traits, values and self concept of the individual (Clardy 2008). Clardy (2008) discuss the work of Spencer and Spencer (1993) who claim that training competence however expanded the focus on skills and knowledge which includes personality traits, increasing the number of variables that could explain and promote job performance as well as shifting emphasis from enabling adequate performance to producing superior ones.

However, competence is based on skills rather than knowledge, in other word; competence training will convince employees of the need to give time and commitment to learning new skill in other to increase their performance and to see their role as accepting these challenges for change (Bramham). Having a well designed and structured competence based training and development program; the organization can work towards ensuring that they have the right skills and the right people to achieve their organizational goals and sustain competitive advantage which can only be achieved by having employees that can effectively and efficiently perform their job (Stensgaard 2004).

Training is believed to improve the knowledge and the skills of the employee as well as change their attitudes toward work which can lead to benefits such as the increase in the confidence, motivation and the commitment of staffs, broaden the opportunity for career progression, give a feeling of personal achievement and satisfaction and help to improve the availability and quality of staffs (Mullins 2002). Training can be a source of motivation development for the employee if it is carried out as a form of support for the employee and in the process of training the employees learns what is expected of them in doing their job and what they need to do better (Thomason 1988).

Learning

One of the functions of Human Resource development is to assist the organization by creating an environment suitable for learning which is required to help develop staffs to meet agreed objectives (Wilson 2005). Learning is defined as "a change in an individual's level of knowledge, skills or attitudes" (Gibb 2008). Learning is believed to be the individual's ability to cope with change which can be acquired either through formal education or training or through informal experiences (Wilson 2005). As much as organizations are interested in ensuring they utilize the knowledge and skills of all their employees it is believed that little is gained through training provided at work but it is believed that most learning acquired by the individual is through their interaction with colleagues, clients which is said to be learning acquired through experience (Mullins 2002).

It is believed that learning and development has helped develop employee's skills in organizations which have prompted employee's performance and lead to organizational success (CIPD 2008). Learning is believed to be linked to behavioral outcomes in other words learning does not only involve what is being taught but making sense of experiences and by doing that learning new skills (Stewart and McGoldrick 1996). Learning at work can be said to be learning for work and it is believed that what people learn will be applied to work in other to support current and future work requirement, also, as learning at work increases the ability of the individual at work so does learning outside work increase the individuals work performance (Megginson et al 1999).

Learning can be beneficial to an organization as well as the individual in the organization by increasing the capacity and the ability of everyone to contribute to the growth of the organization, by developing the individuals skill's and potentials and enabling them to be able to meet the demand of change, also, it provides a solution to organizational issues, enables the organization to meet its goals and produce a wider range of solutions to organizational issues (Mullins 2002).

Development

Development is believed to be a form of learning and training which changes the individual intellectually and not just changing their work skill or knowledge but the individual as a whole and it also helps the individual to grow in their career and also in all aspect of life (Gibb 2008). Development is said to involve preparing the individual in the organization for expected changes in their job or for a future job or a role (Mullins 2002). Development involves the growth of an individual's ability through learning which can be conscious or unconscious (Wilson 2005). Wilson (2005:6) cited the work of Bolton (1995) who points out that "development occurs when a gain in experience is effectively combined with the conceptual understanding that can illuminate it, giving increased confidence both to act and to perceive how such actions relates to its context".

Employee development involves attitude which includes concepts like growth, expansion, improvement, and education (Maund 2001), and also gives the employee opportunity to develop their skills, abilities, realize their potential and to advance their career in or outside the organization (Armstrong 2009), and to change their attitude as a result of going through the process of motivational development (Thomason 1988). Development involves the acquisition of skills which is derived from learning (Thomason

1988).Employee development as wide impact on the individual and not just on the individual but also on the organization and the community in which the organization works (Maund 2001).

Mentoring

"Mentoring is a relationship in which experienced managers aid individuals in the earlier stage of their career and such relationship provides an environment for convening technical, interpersonal and organizational skills from the more experienced to the less experienced" (Mathis and Jackson 2003). Mentoring is seen as a variable in the achievement of success for both the individual and the organization who seek to manage the development of their employees who are the future leaders to engage in order to grow and to develop to senior managers (Gibb 2008). It is believed that mentoring is a form of support in enabling women to progress up the career ladder particular in the area of professions and management (Gibb 2008). "Effective mentors will not only encourage individuals to reflect upon their career goals, thereby promoting a sense of purpose and control they will also help individuals acquire the skills necessary to operate within a less hierarchical structure" (CIPD 2008).

The skills, approaches and the general behavior of the mentor have an important effect on the employee's willingness to learn and also on the commitment shown by the employees towards the learning process (Megginson et al 1999). Also, mentors can serve as a source of motivation for the individual in a way of support in the early stage of their career (Mathis and Jackson 2003). Motivation can be used to aid the employee to give their best to their job or increase their performance in the area of their job or work according to set standards, also, it is believed that people tend to work better if they understand the nature of their job and how they are suppose to carry it out and why they are suppose to carry it out in that particular way (Thomason 1988).

SUSTAINING COMPETITVE ADVANTAGE THROUGH THE WORK OF HUMAN RESOURCE DEVELOPMENT (ORGANIZATION EXAMPLE)

Human resource development is viewed as an important necessity to Walt Disney because to them training is seen as an important investment in the success of their company, while some organizations see training as necessary but expensive, Walt Disney make it top priority (Handout). "Walt Disney believe so strongly in a company's responsibility for training its employees "(handout), and they believe that it is the talent, enthusiasm and the dedication of their employee that has sustained them over the years (Disneyland paris.com). they believe that in other for their employees to perform excellently and not embarrass themselves they need to go through a training program and also need to practice whatever they have been trained on (Handout).

Before starting in their new job their employees go through training program that is based on their profession and what their job entails, in other to develop their skills (Marie). They believe that everyone that works with them from the senior to the junior employer has a right to learn, develop and to grow (Marie). According to them, training, learning and practicing has important roles to play in the in the development of their employees talent and in other for them to perform well they need to be thoroughly trained and also they need to rehearse their roles which lead to the establishment of the Disney university (Hand out).

Disney University is believed to be a training proccss and Walt Disney makes sure that every new employee goes through a training process before starting in their new job and the training process is directed towards imparting knowledge about specific job skills, competencies and also ensures that the employee has a good understanding of the company's culture and tradition (Handout). Their training is based on developing the professional ability and the performance of their employee and they believe that the employees should be able to develop themselves and in turn develop others in the process (Marie).

"At the Disney University student receive complete orientation called Traditions, which includes an explanation of the company's values and traditions, on-the-job training, and procedures for advancement" (Handout). Their employees are also provided with teachers who serve as mentors who has more experience and who can show the employees what should be done and what not to do (handout). The implementation of training in Walt Disney was to train their employees in other to develop their skills, knowledge and their ability and as a result, get the performance needed to be competitive and to sustain a competitive advantage by having the right employees (handout). Walt Disney sees training as the bases for Human resource and as a way of developing their business, their workers and also themselves (Marie).

CONCLUSION

Human resource development has an important role to play in the development of an employee and in the growth of an organization, by providing an organization with the proper employees who have undergone training and learning new skills in other to develop their skills, knowledge, abilities and their competencies

Reference

Armstrong, M. (2009) Armstrong's Handbook of Human Resource Management Practice, 9th edn, Kogan Page, London.

Brumback, G.H (2003) "Blending "we/me" in performance management [Electronic copy], Team performance management, Volume 8, Issue 7/8, Pg 167-173.

Clardy, A. (2008) "Human resource development and the resource based model of core competencies: Methods for diagnosis and assessment" [Electronic copy], Human resource development review, Volume 7, Issue 4, Pg 387-407.

Disneyland Paris (2010) "Corporate responsibility" Disneylandparis.com corporate.disneylandparis.com/corporate-responsibility/our-people/diverse-and-multicultural/cast-member-interviews.xhtml [Accessed 05/04/2010].

Gibb, S. (2008) Human resource development: Processes, Practices and Perspectives, 2nd edn, Palgrave, New York.

Heathfield, S.M. (2010) "What is human resource development (HRD)" About.com humanresources.about.com/od/glossaryh/f/hr_development.htm [Accessed 27/03/2010].

Hunt, J.W, Baruch, Y. (2003) "Developing top managers: the impact of interpersonal skills training", [Electronic copy]. Journal of Management Development, Volume 22, Issue 8, Page 729-752.

Lasbleis, J.M. (2010) "Training" Disneylandparis-casting.com http://disneylandparis-casting.com/en/our-hr-philosophy/training [Accessed 03/04/2010].

Mathis, R.L., Jackson, J.H (2003) Human resource management, 10th edn, Thomson, Ohio.

Megginson, D., Banfield, P., Joy-Mathews, J. (1999) Human Resource development, 2nd edn, Kogan page, London.

Mullins, L.J (2002) Management and organizational behaviour, 6th edn, Pearson education, Harlow.

Philbeam, S., Corbridge, M. (2002) People resourcing: HRM in practice, 2nd edn, Pearson education, Harlow.

Stensgaard, A.B (2007) "Competence based training and Development, Ameinfo.com, www.ameinfo.com/43457.html [Accessed 29/03/2010].

Stewart, J., McGoldrick, J. (1996) Human resource development: Perspectives, strategies and practice, Pearson education, Harlow

Swanson, A.R, Arnold, D.E (1996) "The purpose of human resource development is to improve organizational performance", Richardswanson.com www.richardswanson.com/publications/Swanson(1996)ThePurpose.pdf [Accessed 27/03/2010].

Swanson, R.A. () "Human resource development: performance is the key" cmapspublic.ihmc.us/rid=1217113903859_1440042561_12670/Overview%20of%20HRD%20-%20Swanson.pdf [Accessed 27/03/2010].

Thomason, G. (2003) A text book of human resource management, institute of personal management, London.

Torrington, D., Hall, L., Taylor, S (2005) Human resource management, 6th edn, Pearson education, Harlow.

Willson, J.P. (2005) Human resource development: Learning and training for individuals and organizations, 2nd edn, Kogan page, London.

Internal sources advantages of filling a vacancy internally, they include better motivation because employee capabilities are more ensured to promote or transfe, improved moral, performance and loyalty to the employee, lower staff turnover rate, better utilisation of employees because he/she owns more abilities in a different job or capacity , less training required, greater reliability than external recruitment because a present employee is the terms of personality, attitudes, values, work habits etc. known more, being quicker and cheaper than external recruitment.

External source advantages when the company need to expand and growth contribute to the need for recruitment. Other factors include resignation, dismissal, retirement and relocation. Althougm internal recruitment has many advantages,many positions are filled by external applicants. When an internal candidate is transferred or promoted, it means that his/her position then because a vacancy, presuming that there is no reduction in staff numbers and no organizational restructing. Hence, external recruitment can be time consuming , expensive and uncertain. However, organizations still need to conduct the external sources selecting method on a regular basis. The external recruitment source channels may include internal online or newspaper advertising, private employment agencies, professional bodies appointment services, local employment services office of government labor deparment, direct links with universities, colleges and schools, unsolicited applications, recommendations by present employees or by othe employers' referrals.

Talent management steps in validating a test. Test aims to ensure whether the testee's listening and speaking competence, he/she owns the skilful effort is enough to do the vacancy or position in the organization. The steps in validating a test is as below:

The organization needs to analyze the job. It is necessary to conduct a careful job analysis to produce a good job description and an appropriate job specification. These requirements can then become the objectives of the selection tests. Then, it needs to choose the test from among the various testing means, choose the one that is the most valid and reliable. Next, it needs to administer the test. One can either tesst current employees and find out of there is any significant differences between the scores and the employees' performances , it means concurrent validation or test potential candidates before they are hired and compare their scores with their performances after they have been in their jobs, it means predictive validation.

However, predictive validation may have disadvantages, e.g. job performance may be difficult to assess objectively, the process of validation may be lengthy, the results of the test are compared with the performance of a selected group only, it is not completely validated. Concurrent validation is quick, but its disadvantages may include standardisation is difficult, the test is validated against a non-typical group only, i.e. present employers rather than candidates for employment, the present employe may not behave normally when they do the test.

Reference

Marion, D. & Michel, S. (2014) the economist, Managing talent, Profile books ltd, London, UK, pp.1-2, 6.

Marion, D. & Michel, S. (2014) explained talent is the sum of a person's abilities, his or her intrinsic grifts, skills, knowledge, experience, intelligenc, judgement, attitude, character and drive. It also includes his or her ability to learn. At the international level, talent shortages are more severe. During the past decade, an internationally mobile group of employees, who can pick and choose where they work. As firms in employing markets also begin competing in the global economy, these people are in ever-greater demand. For example, Sinapore has had on an intensive recruitment programme for skilled foreigh workers, with more liberal criteria for eligibility to work in the country. Some 90,000 now work in the city-state, the majority from the US, UK, France, Australia, Japan and South Korea.

Marion, D. & Michel, S. (2014) indicated several factors need to be takne into account to understand the market for skilled labour. Hays and Oxford Economics pooled their data to identify seven

components that together give a better picture of skill shortages as below:
labour-market participation means the degree to which a country's talent pool is fully utilised, for example, whether women and older workers have access to jobs; labour -market flexibility means the legal and regulatory environment is faced by business, especially how easily immigrants can fill talent gaps; wage pressure overall means whether real wages are keeping pace with inflation; wage pressure in high-skill industries means which wages in high-skill industries outpace those in low-skill industries; wage pressure in high-skill occupations means rises in wages for highly skilled workers are a short -term indicaton of skills shortages, talent mismatches means the mismatch between the skills are needed by businesses and those available, are indicated by the number of long-term unemployed and job vacancies; educational flexibility means whether the educational system can adapt to meet the future needs of organizations for talent, especially in the fields of mathematics and science.
Firms operating in knowledge-intensive industries depend on their most capable staff to help create value through intangible assets, such as patents, licences and technical know-how. In fact, globalisation and technological competition brings to much complexity of many jobs and occupations. Firms are now looking for individuals with an range of abilities that might include specialized skills, broader functional skills, industry expertise and knowledge of specific geographical markets. The skills include: digital skill means the fast growing digital economy is increasing the demand for highly skilled technical workers. Companies are looking for staff with social-media based skills, especially in " digital expression". Agile thinking means the regulatory and environment uncertainty, such as life sciences and energy and mining industry's talent knowledge, ability skill is needed for employee's personal effort and characteristic needs; interpersonal and communication skill, H R managers predict that co-creativity and brainstorming skills be greatly in demand, it will bring relationship building and

teamwork skills; global operating skill means that ability to manage diverse employee is seen as the most important global operating skill,, glocalisation (where home-market products and services are tailored to the taste of overseas customers and innovation (where staffs lead innovation and then the company applies these new ideas to mature markets).

Talent is a relative concept, it includes these components, such as technical specialists, especially in areas key to the organization's core capabilities, individuals with hard-to-recurit skills, bright individuals from underrepresented groups whom the positions , the best-performing graduates or school leavers and managers with the potential to move into senior mangement positions at the local, national or internatonal level. However, judgement effort is the main factor to influence organizations to select individuals whose behavior and values fit with those of the organization. How performance and potential are measured is for senior managers to decide.

In many cases, the definition of exceptional performance is explained in competency frameworks and appraisal systems. Defining high potential can be more difficult and might include a range of assessment tools, such as development centres, psychometric testing and the personal judgement of those whose insights into talent are widely repected.

Talent plan has three components: talent gaps mean HR works with business management levels. Once a year to identify which leadership , management and functional skills are needed, how those roles and responsibilities and whether the talent processes are producing people who will be able to solve these skill gaps; talent supply means most of the focus is on management trainees and a smaller porportion of people who are recurited mid-career; talent development means recruiting high-potential individuals at the start of their careers and taking them through a structured development programme.

Talent strategy means how senior leaders can identify the capabilities that help achieve the company's strategy strategic objectives and provide a competitive effort. These capabilities are not just tactical or operational skills, which although important, do have as much of an impact on business performance and profit. Operational management or senior levels and the talent management team then break down each capabilities into parts, such as specific skills, knowledge and expertise. They look at how these skills sets enable each business unit to deliver their part of the strategic plan.

This analysis should indicate the roles where knowledge and expertise are needed for maximum business value. There are not automatically senior leadership or management values. They also extend to technical and specialist roles or to previously overlooked roles, e.g. positions within the organization that help sure that expertise from one part of the business. Part of review many necessitate a fresh look at knowledge management processes across the business. The HR team should also review its own ways of working and thinking o make sure that its processes for recruitment, selection, learning and development, appraisal , reward and recognition and concentrates on the skills, cultural values and behaviors most critical to business performance.

Talent review aims to assess how well employees are performing currently in the critical roles, identified by the strategic review, and their potential to move into more demanding roles. Some of the required data will be held centrally by HR, but almost certainly, the team carrying out the review will need to speak directly to operational and line managers to get feedback about the performance and potential of key individuals.

At part of the review, gap analysis will help identify gaps in skills necessary to carry out the business's strategy and plans and whether any critical roles are unfilled. Succession planning is a important factor here as it may well be that insufficient numbers of potential successors have been identified for certain critical roles. A talent based gap analysis main aim is to focus on hiring and/ or training needs as part of a talent strategy, it is the company's strategic planning process. It draws ona wide source of data, both

internally and externally. It looks at strategic needs both current and future, and makes judgements about operational needs.
This analysis determines whether the right talented people are in the right position at the right time. These three factors will influence whether talent planning needs to be improved. For example, right people, but wrong time, it means that people who might not be being used currently because of ao downturn in markets, but who the organization does not want to lose as it takes too much time and money to replace them when demand increases. The organization must therefore determine its strategy for retaining and motivating them; wrong people means that people are not employed to perform the work .
This suggests that a mistake is between HR processes and the business strategy, learning and development processes may not be keeped good with changing business needs. There may be needed to appraise and promote to make right decisions that are leading to a mismatch between roles and people, right people, but wrong location. It means that people who can do the work , but are in the wrong location as a result of a reorganization and constraints on mobility, make more creative use of temporary assignments and virtual working, or relocate work to where it can be done by the most skilful employees.
Finally, once the talent review has identified any shortagesof talent, an organization has three options: either buying talent through external recuritment or building talent through tailored learning and development programmes that involve work experiences that will help talent employment development or borrowing talent by resorting to temporary workers or outsourcing.
Buying talent is an obvious choice when a company needs particular skills or expertise that it does not have time or ability ro develop in existing staff is to buy in that talent. The task is then to source this expertise, and offer the right set of inducements to recruit and retain individuals with the desired skills. However, buying talent can be costly as the going rate for sought-after specialists is high and they are often in a strong negotiating

position. For example, swift recuritment processes and flexible remuneration package can attract talent employees‘ applications through external recuritment seeking recritment method.

Borrowing talent is a temporary need for specialist skills it makes sense to borrow or " rent" what is required by contracting with, for example, freelancers, independent consultants, staff on seondment or firms that will supply staff. This form of flexible labour means uncertain times such flexibility becomes more attractive because it enables firms to assemble new combinatins of skills in swift reponse to sudden shifts in their environment. It provides firms with access to wider pool of talent, especially in the case of work that can be performed in any location.

Building talent means that a larger firm will seek to build its own talent by creating a reliable high potential and high performing employees. The aim is to rise and train talent skilful employees' qualities and efforts and to invest in their careers in the expectation that they will progress to senior positions in the business. So, these individuals are placed in a talent pool where their progress is monitored and where they are given extra opportunities for training and development. To keep talented people to develop, there is an emphasis on performance management, so any weakness or developments are needed to find.

CHAPTER III

The relationship between social change and human behavior

Human Behavioral network job brings social economic benefits

What does human network job mean ? Why may human network job be popular? Why human network job behavior may influence economy ?

Nowadays internet is popular to use. We can apply internet to find data , search any new things, even earn money. Why does internet may become huma network job source. For example, e-publish may be one kind of new human network job. Any authors may apply internet

channel to help them to sell electronic or paper books from e-publisher web store. They may apply facebook, you tub etc. any online

channel to promote themselves new books to let new readers to know whether when they may buy themselves favourable new topic books to read

from electronic publisher web store.

Thus, future electronic publisher industry may help any authors to build internet network platform to help them to sell and promote ot advertise their any one new electronic or paper book topic to let global any one reader to choose to buy their any new topic books from electronic publisher web store easily and conveniently. However, it implies that electronic network platform author may be one kind of future new human network job in our societies.

How electronic network platform author job may bring economy benefit in macro economy view? A person can have few friends, contacts and still be very influential if these few friends and contacts are themselves highly influential, e.g. one author must not need to know any one reader in global society. When they like to choose any electronic books from electronic internet network platform. They may become the author's any one topic book buyer, when they feel the author's any one topic book is fun and attract they make decision to buth the strange author whose the topic book from electronic book publisher's platform web store conventiently in short time. Although, they are strangers, they do not know themselves , but the reader can understand what it way that made Google from writing platofrm to create new creative mind and typing network job method to replace traditional hand writing book method for global authors. It will be one kind of new human network writing job.

Hence, global any one reader can apply an innovative search engine , such as google.com to find whether whom author personal new topic books are value to read from internet.
Then, the electroniuc publisher's web store may be new book store platform sale network to help the author to sell many electronic or paper books from electronic network platform
in short time. So, internet may be future new network plaform to help global any one author to create network writing job absolutely. Furthermore, internet may be popular social media
to help any one author to build goold relationship between his/her readers. It is one kind of new network, human network job. New authors do not need to buy many paper books to prepare to put in any one book shop warehouse. Their every book can print on demand to reduce out of book stock in any one book shop. They may choose to sell either electronic books or paper books both from any one book publisher web store. So, electronic network platform may be one kind of good writing channel to help human authors to create income and it can also help authors to bring new creative mind and new topic fun content books to let readers to know and buy to read from electronic publisher network platform.

Why does human behavior may be one kind of new human network job to bring global economic advantages. ALthough, it may be free income or without inocme, but the person does the network behavior, his/her behavior may be bring advantages to influence many other people's health. For this case, when a worker in a coffee shop in an airport gets a vaccination aganinst the flu, it does not only helps him or her stay healthy, but also helps the many travellers who might otherwise have been inflected if that workers caught the flu. So, the externality , the result implies the vaccination of even a part of a community conveys benefits to the whole community. For example, governments pay special attention to the vaccinations of school children, teachers, health mothers, and the elderly, categories of people particularly susceptible not only to catching, but also to transmitting a disease.

It is not accidential that governments are heavily involved with vaccination . When there are externalities, free market, fail to persuade individual incentives with society's
their the worker's decision of whether to get a vaccine ends up attracting whether other people get sick. The workers might not fully take all these other people's potential suffering into account when making her or his vaccination decision.

As Stanford University does many suggestions, understand this and tries to help them make the right decisions and so providers free flu vaccines for its staff and students.

Small pockets of unvaccinated individuals can allow a disease to gain a spread more widely well-being. For example, parent weighing the costs and benefits of a vaccine for their child is not always thinking of the consequences of that vaccination to other people. THese are markets in which subsidizing or regulating behavior can make everyone better off. Because the reason for requiring that a child be vaccinated before enrolling in school is not just to protect that child, because each child's vaccination affects others via potential contagions.

Robots take our jobs behavioral and economy influences

Robot job behavior brings economy influences

If one day robots can replace human to do simple, even complex jobs. They will bring what influences to our global societial economy.The popular economic refrain declares that the global middle class is dying and robots will soon take our jobs, e.g. shopping center customer service jobs, library service jobs, cinema ticket sale jobs, restaurant kitchen cooker jobs, even, bus drivers, taxi drivers etc. public transport driving jobs, accountant, doctors etc. professional jobs. Whether it is beautiful or petty matter if our future societies have many human jobs can be replaced to do from robots. Businessman must may reduce to employ employees and reduce to pay salary or wage, when robots can be replaced to do their employees tasks. But, societies must bring unemployement rate rises , due to societies will have many people loss jobs when their employers choose to buy robots to serve their clients or do any office tasks or customer service or cleaning etc. tasks.

In micro economy view, employers may save money in long term, but in macro economy view, it will cause unemployment ratio rises , even crime rate rises when there are many people lose jobs in societies. These models of doom, though, fail to account for the hundreds of businesses riding the waves of change in their industries when robots may be invented to replace human to do many simple , even complex tasks in our future societies.

WE may image that one small factory needs to manufacture fishes canes to sell to supermarket, the small , cheaper stuff and higher margin parts of the fishes manufacture industry. Before, this factory needs to employe many human factory workers need to help every fresh customer makeing the perfect fishing gear, designed for performance, durability, and cost in order to achieve to manufacture every fish cane in whole fished processing manufacturing stages. Every worker needs to spend about 15 to twenty minutes to finish every fish cane , till to delivery to any supermarket to sell. If this fish canes manufacturing factory can apply manufacturing robots to help them to finish any one working tasks , every robot can only spend five minutes to finish whole fresh fish cane manufacturing process. Thus, every robot can

help this factory save 10 to 15 minutes time to finsh every fish cane manufacturing process. IN fact, time is money, because when every robot can help this factory to reduce 10 to 15 minutes time to compare human worker. Then, this factory can finish about 20 fish canes in one hour if it can use robot to help it to manufacture fish canes. Otherwise, if this factory still use human workers to help it to manufacture fish canes, then it can finsh about 3 to 4 fish canes in one hour. SO, the manufacturing efficiency ensures that robots must help this fish manufacturing factory to raise fish canes number more than human workers. So, in robotic behavioral economy view, manufacturing robots must help this fish canes manufacturing factory to raise fish canes manufacturing number and deliver increasing number to supermarkets to prepare to sell every day. Robots can help this fish canes manufacturing factory bring manufacturing time saving, rising manufacturing efficiency, improving performance and reducing wages expenditure long time advantages in micro economy view. However, manufacturing robots can also bring disadvanages to society, e.g. increasing unemployment ratio, increasing crime rate,
this factory workers will lose jobs and income, they need earn social welfare from government and increasing government finance pressure in short time, even long time in macro economic view.

Stanford University graduate program in economics, Scott lecturer explained that "in demand and supply economic theory for robots supply and demand case, robots supply number increasing may influence human workers demand number decrease. It sometimes calls " the efficient frontier".
No specific human beings were mentioned in any of economics classes. As robots supply and demand in market case, They (robots) may be purely theoretical " agents" who reached to the most reasonable sale prices in order to persuade any one businessman buyer to make manufacturing robot buying decision whether robots can help him / her to bring how much saving time , saving money, saving cost, improving performance, efficiency economic benefit before he/she plans to reduce workers number when he/she

decides to apply robots to replace human workers in his/her factory or office or any service department, e.g. cinema ticket sale service, shopping center customer service, shopping center cleaning , supermarket customer service etc. service or sale tasks. When robots can replace human to do any one of these tasks in any organizations. So, robots may be human worker agents who reached to prices the way robots would react to a software command. There was nothing that explained why some people thrived and others did n't or why truly brilliant, hardworking people could fail when much lazier folks succeeded." Having been admitted to the Stanford University graduate program in economics, Scott lecturer hoped to get his answers there.

How robots influence our future social changing? Using the right technology can be a boon to your business in this economy. For internet example, it is easier than ever to find well-matched customers all around the world, to stay in contact with them, and to more quickly design the products they want. If you focus solely on being cutting -edge, though you risk letting the technology take over what should be very robust relationships with your customers , employees, and colleagues. IN nowaddays society, technoligical advances and cutomation, personal relationships in business are more crucial than ever. I mean that robots can not replace human to serve clients to let them to feel more comfortable and passion more easily. For shoe shop case example, if the shoe shop apply one robot to serve its clients to replace human shoe salesperson to serve its shoe customers. Robots ensure that they can not persuade every shoe potential buyer to make shoe buying decision more easily when robots need to contact every shoe potential buyer. The reason is simple, because robots can not touch any one shoe buyer individual emotion very easier.
If the shoe buyer needs the robots to help him/her to choose any right shoe styles when he/she can not feel himself / herself can make the most right shoe style choice decision. The robots can not replace human shoe salesperson to make shoe style choice judgement more easily. They must need longer time to analyze

whether which shoe style may be the most suitable to the shoe buyer. Otherwise, human shoe salesperson may attempt to make the most right shoe style choice decision to help any one shoe buyer to chooce the most right style shoe because he/she owns shoe style sale experience, shoe style knowledge, the most important reason is that they can feel every shoe customer individual emotion to touch whether he/she will feel comfortable or happy when they attempt to help every shoe customer to seek the most right shoe style in every shoe customer whole shoe searching processing. Othwerwise, serving robots are only one machine, they can not touch or feel every shoe customer individual emotion whether he/she feel comfortable or unhappy or happy when they need to contact them in whole shoe searching processing. Hence, I believe that some tasks robots can

not repalce human staff to do very easily. Otherwise, robots may bring disadvanatges to let any one businessman to loss his/her customers, due to robots can not touch every customer

emotion to compare human staff in service tasks more easily. Robots serving customer behaviors may cause money lose and customers number lose to the shop in micro economic view.

Intellectual human economic behaviors

What does intellectual human economic behaviors mean ? I believe that when we choose or decide to do intellectual behaviors, then our societies will be influenced to bring economic growth in consequence.I shall attempt to indicate pollution case to explain how and why eithet our intellectual or foolish behaviors may bring economic growth or recession in consequence as below:

On one hand, for air pollution social case aspect example, if we only consider to buy cars to drive for working aimr or holiday leisure aim. Then, our societies air will be polluted. Our health will be influenced to bad. Our car driving behaviors may cause global environment air pollution serously. In long tiem, global air pollution will bring our bodies health to be bad. Although, ourselves car driving behaviors may bring our driving travelling leisure enjoyment and comfortable feeling in short time, also we so not need to pay public transport fare often, but we need to compensate ourselves health economic intangible loss due to air pollution , when cars number increases, dirty air will cause ouselves health to become bad.

In the result, we will need to pay more medical expenditure when we are old age, due to ourselves bodies will become bad, due to we breathe global dirty air every day, due to ourselves cars pollute air in long time, e.g. 10 to 20 years, even 30 more without limited air pollution environment. So, driving cars behavior may be one kind of human foolish behavior and our foolish behavior may bring ourselves future long time medical expenditure absolutely.

One the other hand, water pollution social aspect, if we often keep much rubblish to pollute sea, oil exploration porcessing pollute ocean , ships gas pollute ocaen, then fishes will eat polluted food and drive dirty water, due to global ocean is polluted.

In fact, because human only to conside how to buy boats to carry on leisure enjoyment activities, or catch cruises to travel on the sea. Also, oil manufacturers only consider researching anywhere to find new oil exploration places to manufacture oil product, when their oil exploration processes pollute ocarn . Consequently, global fishes drink polluted warer or eat polluted food. They will have poison. SO, human will have high chance to eat poison polluted fishes, due to fishes are poison or are polluted.

So, human is doing foolish activities, we only hope to find oil exploration places to pollute ocean or we only spend money to buy ticket to catch ships to travel anywhere in global ocean. All of these human foolish behaviors will bring pollution to global ocean. On consequently, we will need to compensate to eat polluted or dirty or poision fishes, ourselves bodies health will be bad. In long time, we need have high chance to pay medical expenditure when we are old. So, pollution case may be one good example to explain how and why human foolish behavior may influence ourselves future need to compensate serious medical loss.

All of these human foolish behavior will bring pollution to global ocean. On consequently, we will need to compensate to eat polluted or dirty or poison fished , ourselves bodies health will be bad. In long time, we will have high chance to pay medical expenditure, when we are old. So, pollution case may be one good example to explain how and why human ourselves intellectual or foolish behaviors may influence future long time economic loss or economic growth or recession in micro and micro economic view.

On another water pollution aspect hand, if we often keep rubbish to sea, oil exploration processing pollutes ocean and ships' gas pollute ocean, then fishes will eat polluted food and drink dirty water, due to fishes will eat polluted food and drink dirty sea water because the global ocean is polluted seriously.

In fact, because human only consider how to buy boats to carry on any leisure water activities, or catches cruises to travel on the sea. Also, oil manufacturers only consider any where to find oil exploratin places to manufacture oil products from ocean, when their pol exploration processes can plooute ocean. Consequently, global fishes drink polluted water or eat direty food. They will have poison. So, human will have high chance to eat poison fishes.

Otherwise, such as pollutin case, it can infuence inflation or deflation. Consequently, the reason indicates supply and demand theory. If air pollution is serious, then we will consider health issue, global cars demand number may be influenced to reduce, when global cars number demand will reduce, global car prices and supply number will need to change to fall down in order to attract or persuade global car consumers choose to make car purchase decision.

Hence, global car manufacture number and car price will be influenced to reduce, due to global air pollution issue. Consequently, deflation will occur because when the country citizen usually does not spend much extra saving money to buy car expensive goods. Money value will be low. Otherwise, if global cair pollution is not serious, human considers to buy cars to enjoy driving leisure lives. So, global car demand is influenced to increase , also global car price will also influenced to increase.

Consequently, gobal human will choose to buy cars to drive. Due to we accept to spend extra saving to buy expensive car goods. Car sale price and supply may be influenced to rise up. Money value is influenced to reduce. Inflation may be influenced, due to global car consumers number increases, we would not have extra money to spend easily. Car expensive goods expenditure influences our spending habit to avoid to make car purchase decision more easily. So, human intellectual or foolish activities may bring inflation or deflation consequency in possible indirectly in macro economic view.

On conclusion, above pollution case explain that how and why human intellectual or foolish economic behaviors may bring inflation or deflation consequency as wll as economic growth or recession consequency as well as any goods demand and supply increasing or decreasing consequency. It implies that human behavior may have indirect relationship to influence any goods demand and supply number to either increase or decrease result as well as any goods price will be influenced to increase or decrease in micro and macro economic view.

The relationship between social change and human behavior

Why does economic changes may influence human individual behavioral change? I shall attempt to indicate shopping behavior and staying at home behavior to explain their case and effect relationsip as below:

Human behavior can be influenced by economic change or economic change can be influenced by human behavior? Why does recession may influence consumers reduce shopping desire? In social recession suitation, it is possible that many people lose jobs suddenly, due to businessmen lose many customers. They need to make decision to reduce employees number in order to continue to keep businesses. Consequently, many firms (organizations) their employees may lose jobs. When they have much time, due to lose jobs, they will feel to avoid to spend too much time and money to go to shopping often. Many losing jobs people, they will often stay at homes.

So, they will reduce time to go to shopping, then non essential

products won't their preferable choice purchase products. Hence, recession will change many losing jobs people their shopping or consumption desires to avoid to buy non essential products often . Usually when economic boom, many people have jobs to do because consumers number must increase when many people have jobs to do. Then, many people can accept to spend money to buy non essential products often. Many people feel spend time to go to shopping can satisfy their purchase of any kinds of new products useful psychology or desire. So, recession is one good example to explain it can influence many people do not like often to leave homes to go to shopping easily. Many people like to stay at homes, becaue they feel worry about spending too much shopping time when they leave homes. Their staying home time is one good negative shopping behavior example. So, economic change may influence human individual behavior changes , they have direct cause and efect relationship in behavioral economic view.
May human behavior influence economic change? Is it possible that human behavior may bring the country social economic change in macro economic or micro behavioral economic view ? I shall indicate publishing industry example. Do you feel that if there are many students feel learning is very important when they read many books or many of students feel interesting to read or they have reading new books in habit, then it is possible that the country will have many students like to spend time to go to any book shops to choose the books, they feel that they can help they learn new knowledge. Then the country will increase students number, they often spend time to visit any one book shop every week. Their visiting book shops behavior which may become their habits. So, the country will increase students number, they often spend time to visit book shops. Also, it implies that visiting book shops behaviors may be their behavioral habits.
So, when the country has many students often spend time to visit book shops , their visiting book shops behaviors may help any one book shop to raise books sale chance. So, the country's student individual often visiting book shop behaviors, their habitual visiting

book shops behaviors must may assist help any one book shop to increase books sale number absolutely.
Consequently, any one book shop , its books sale bumber must be influenced to increase to increase because the country will have many students like or feel need visit book shops habit in order to choose any suitable books to buy to read at home in order to raise themselves learning effort. When the country has many bok shops often have many students visit their book shops, then their books sale number may be influenced to increase. It explain why student individual visiting book shop behavior may help any one book shop sale number increases also.

Printed by Libri Plureos GmbH in Hamburg,
Germany

9 798887 838342